WORM-EATEN TIME

POEMS FROM A LIFE
UNDER NORMALIZATION

1968–1989

BY PAVEL ŠRUT

Translated by
Deborah Garfinkle

Phoneme Media
1551 Colorado Blvd., Suite 201
Los Angeles, California 90041

First Edition, 2016

ISBN: 978-1-939419-61-3

Library of Congress Control Number: 2015959970

This book is distributed by Publishers Group West

Cover art by Ron Morosan
Cover design by Jaya Nicely
Design and typesetting by Scott Arany

Printed in the United States of America

Phoneme Media is a nonprofit publishing and film production house, a
fiscally sponsored project of Pen Center USA, dedicated to disseminating
and promoting literature in translation through books and film.

http://phoneme.media

Curious books for curious people.

WORM-EATEN TIME

POEMS FROM A LIFE
UNDER NORMALIZATION

1968–1989

BY PAVEL ŠRUT

Translated by
Deborah Garfinkle

PHONEME
MEDIA
Los Angeles

Publication of this book was made possible in part by generous grants from the PEN American Center and The National Endowment for the Arts

Some of these poems have appeared in the following journals and magazines to whose editors I wish to express my many thanks: Two Lines, TriQuarterly, B O D Y, *and* The Massachusetts Review.

*To Pavel with love, admiration
and the deepest gratitude.*

Worm-Eaten Time:
The Ghetto Wall that Normalization Built

IT IS DEEPLY IRONIC THAT THE TERM *NORMALIZATION* REP-
resents the period of Czech history that began a short
while after the Soviet tanks crushed the life out of
Prague Spring in August 1968, lasting until 1989's
Velvet Revolution thawed communism's deep chill.
After the tanks of August arrived, nothing about life
in Czechoslovakia during that time was normal;
indeed, the social, cultural, and political fabric of the
time belied any possible sense of normalcy. Alexander
Dubček had been whisked off to Moscow at Leonid
Brezhnev's behest and forced to resign staring at the
end of the proverbial Kalashnikov. In April 1969, Gustáv
Husák was installed as Party Leader by Moscow, mark-
ing the sudden termination of Dubček's vision of *social-
ism with a human face*. It was this liberalizing vision that
had engendered the Prague Spring and its burgeoning
of freedom that had swept across Czechoslovakia, her-
alding a new era like the sprays of delicate apple blos-

soms, covering the flanks of Prague's Petřín Hill in April. Writer Jan Neruda, in the nineteenth century, had once described the apple orchard—its fleeting beauty is the sign that winter's frigid hold on Bohemia has, once again, thankfully, come to an end. And in the endless progression of the seasons, from birth to maturity to death and resurrection, where the flowers once bloomed to be scattered to the wind, the fruit ripened and matured to fall to earth and be buried under the winter snow. So the endless cycle of birth and death would begin again.

But in 1968, the fall no longer brought the promise that spring would rise again from the ashes of the year before it. April 1969 was truly *the cruelest month* because the Iron Curtain had once again rung down on openness. Czechoslovakia hunkered down for the duration bathed in normalization's unnatural twilight. This period, in a sense, metamorphosed into the Kafkaesque world of that spring turned on its head. It was the time in a land where the social fabric had been ripped in two; a country where no one could ever be sure when a purely innocent remark might be taken out of context by a friend, family member, lover, or colleague and reported to the Czech version of the secret police, the Státní bezpečnost, (StB). Nobody knew if they were being watched—if the StB's spies were lurking in the shadows, waiting for the right words to land the speaker an *invitation* to the secret police's main headquarters on Prague's Bartolomějská Street for an interrogation, and possibly a lengthy prison term. After his early literary successs, which took place during the cultural flowering under Dubček during the Prague Spring, the resulting suppression and censorship devastated Šrut, the twenty-eight-year-old poet, whose early career had held so much promise until the Iron Curtain came hurtling down.

It is the eerie eponymous *worm-eaten light* that illuminates Šrut's harrowing meditation of the devastation wrought by the Soviet tanks. The mysterious and otherworldly light casts its sickly pall across the landscape inhabited by goblins, ghouls, and the unnamed malevolent *you* that lurks in the interstices of these haunting poems. Written in the half year after the invasion, *Worm-Eaten Light* is Šrut's "Wasteland." The ghost of Eliot, whom Šrut had studied as a student of English and Spanish at Charles University, haunts the dimly lit reaches of the dying garden where Europe's ruins have morphed into the Czech countryside. These poems unfold from just days after the Soviet invasion, a few short weeks after Šrut returned from an extended stay in England. The collection continues through December, through the depths of winter brought on by the worms—harbingers of death, tiny creatures eating their way through the light with their rapacious appetites. By December 1968, the evidence that spring would not be returning had become increasingly apparent. At the end of August, Czechoslovakia's history had been irrevocably altered and the civil liberties and openness that came with the Prague Spring would not, in the coming months, return again, because nature's cycle had been disrupted by the Siberean winds from the East.

Yet, despite all signs to the contrary, the cycle continued, even behind the high walls in normalization's lonely ghetto. Slowly, imperceptively, after many years of pressure, cracks began to appear. A faint light sputtered and flickered in the street lamps, exposing the house of cards behind the gray prefab housing blocks, and the daisies that had managed to push their way through the permafrost emerged from between the fissures in the concrete. During the slow thaw, Šrut's voice finally returned to him, but transformed, his aspect unfamiliar; the beautiful lyric tenor had morphed into the toad's hoarse croaking. The poet's once handsome visage, now the uncle of the underground ugly mug. It is this poet who speaks to us in *Paperbound Poems*, whose selections all originally appeared in samizdat, unofficially published and circulated in carbon copy among friends and colleagues. The astonishing poems in this collection testify to the fact that the rules of the game were no longer being dictated by the officials with their big ears, prying eyes and endless interrogations. The sadistic playground bullies who taunted Šrut to get him to join their vicious circle in *Worm-Eaten Light* can no longer find their victim. He's already somewhere else, playing hide-and-seek in the ghetto, escaping their banal tyranny by camouflaging himself between the lines of his verse. From this intimate place, he thumbs his nose at their order and pokes fun at himself and the world with a humor that belies normalization's brute reality.

In the end, despite the fear, loneliness, and despair, Šrut and poetry prevail over normalization; the poems, forged out of equal parts laughter and grief, shine with a new beauty, intimacy and truth. And while we leave Šrut waiting at the pub, beer in hand, for the ghetto wall to come crashing down on his head, we know when it eventually falls in November 1989 it will crush the jailor that had devised normalization's terrible architecture, instead of the poets, artists, and dreamers. The poems in *Worm-Eaten Light* and *Paperbound Poems* provide the compelling evidence that the light of spring had once again returned; the velvet season that marked his homeland's transition back to freedom after, to borrow from Šrut's brilliant metaphor, the worm-eaten time.

Deborah Garfinkle
San Francisco, October 2015

A Note on the Translation

HOW TO BE A FAITHFUL TO THE INTENT OF THE ORIGINAL in another language is always the question that plagues the mind of any translator. This is especially true when it comes to poetry, where each choice of word bears an enormous weight within the fabric of the work and each choice about the lyric, rhyme, and meter doubly so. Czech is a language whose fluid syntax and case structure lends itself easily to rhyme; you can twist Czech in a hundred directions and it will still somehow manage to come out in a lovely lyrical bow—end-stopped and neat as a package. English prosody relies on music of a different kind because of its irregularity and final consonants. Internal rhyme frees the words from the harsh rigidity of the end break; in slant rhyme, we feel the glimmer of a symmetry turned askew, a flawed perfection, doubly beautiful because of its failure to fall into the bad habit of being too pretty for its own good.

How to marry these two disparate traditions, given the difference in the linguistic structure and literary conventions of Czech and English, has always been the most difficult part of my work—whether to sacrifice the precision of an image for the sake of preserving the pattern of rhyme or vice versa. No work exists in a vacuum. Every poem embodies a history that lives in each reading, which is specific to the poet's aesthetic, literary conventions, and the time itself. In all cases, the alchemy of translation necessitates a loss—sometimes the choice between the lesser of two evils—or a suitable compromise. The alternative would be to give up and not translate at all, which would be, to my mind, the real failure—the ignorance of the other, which so enriches our imaginations and lives once we have been introduced. But how to make the introduction?

Many years ago my dear friend Jiřina, my cultural guide to all things Czech from the moment I landed in Bohemia, chided me when I told her that I was going to use free verse to translate a poet who so clearly relied on rhyme as much as image to make meaning. I explained that end-stopped rhyme sounded more like children's verse and cheap greeting cards to the ears of an English speaker—that if I tried to reproduce the rhyme, readers would not find the work poetic—they would think it naïve or unpolished despite the rhyme being linguistically complex. She and I argued this point for a long while, but I felt I was completely justified in my view because I assumed, on some level, that readers wouldn't be capable of getting past the aesthetics of English to appreciate the design of the original Czech and embrace its otherness. In the years since, I've learned from my work as a translator, critic, and scholar of Czech that, as usual, Jiřina was right. Abandoning rhyme would be delivering readers pale imitations of the poet's work whose originality had been completely solipsized by the imperialism of my English-language aesthetics—an poor, enslaved copy of the real thing.

In this case, being faithful to Pavel's lyricism, as well as his imagery, has an even more immediate importance in the context of this particular work. Since *Worm-Eaten Time*'s meaning is embodied by Pavel's aesthetic transformation as a result of the external force exerted on his whole being during normalization, not to reproduce this change would be to miss the entire point. The rhyme, word play, and nonsense (influenced by his work in translating English children's verse and nursery rhymes) became Pavel's means to resist the political repression exerted by the Communist authorities. These structural transformations became his means to break the chains that had bound him since the tanks rolled over his homeland. By abandoning his previous manifestation as a lyric poet, Pavel became an ironic master who could escape those who would have mastered him. Thus, without my attempting to reproduce the rhyme, the poems—especially in *Paperbound Poems*—would lose their significance and power. As a result, I have tried wherever and whenever possible to preserve both image and rhyme in order to be faithful to Pavel's freedom to resist the silence and pay tribute to a poet I deeply admire and love as a friend. To do any less would fail to do justice to his power as a poet and the power of poetry to triumph over tyranny and meaninglessness.

ČERVOTOČIVÉ SVĚTLO

WORM-EATEN
LIGHT

ZNAMENÍ

SRPEN–PROSINEC
1968

SIGNS

AUGUST–DECEMBER
1968

U TRATI PES
souká se do králičí kůže. Mráz
zvedá krajinu s praštící
pumpou na řetězu, krajina

Obrací naběhlý jazyk
hlíny. Ještě slámu
prokvetlou v hladkých útrobách
králíka, vnitřnosti

Z povřísla, a tvé oči,
pamatuji. V očích
jen krajina. Odněkud
zhloubi váží vodu.

BY THE TRACKS, A DOG
climbs into the skin of a rabbit. Frost
lifts the countryside with
a chain pump's snapping, the countryside

Turns over the dirt's swollen
tongue. I still remember
straw blooming
in the slick entrails of the rabbit,

The guts, straw-stuffed
and your eyes. In them
nothing but land. They weigh water
from somewhere in the deep.

TAK U NÁS. JEMNĚ
mne podpírají jablkem.
V červí chodbičce hlavu
zvednu. Sytím se

Otrubami. Polykám z nože
mléko ohryzku.
Na lískách: popel
jablečných odkrojků.

Pod hliněným nebem otec
odklopal s prsou
trávu. Vrásní se slupka
jádra, budeme

Tedy zítra česat jablka
z hlíny. Budeme svlékat hořká
jádra po večerech, po
nocích ulíváme vosk.

V červí chodbičce lišaj
vzlétá. Slyším je:
teprve se prořezávají
zuby, kterými stiskneš.

AT OUR PLACE, THEY
gently prop me up with an apple.
In a wormhole
I raise my head. I stuff myself

Full on the bran. I swallow the core's milk
from the apple blades.
On the crates: The ash
of the parings.

Under an earthen sky my father
kicked the grass away
from his breast. The seed's hull
shrivels. So tomorrow

We'll gather apples up
from the dirt. Evening after evening
we'll shuck the bitter seeds. Night after
night we'll pour off the candle wax.

In a wormhole a sphinx moth
takes off. I hear your teeth:
the ones you'll bite me with
as soon as they erupt.

LOŇSKOU KOSTŘIČKOU
ptáka, chyceného
křovím provívá vzduch
a dým. Mezi bílou

Zdí je oheň
nízký, ještě stéká
voda z měkkých hub. Ještě
protáčí, břichem a boky,

Pes lůžko v jalovci.
V rybničném bahnu, opodál,
leží, pohozeno,
tvrdé hnízdo, znak.

Pomalu, zespod. Nasakuje
vodou, roste: nemotorná
bezkřídlá larva, mezi bílou zdí
a bílým peřím,

Kde oheň nízký.

THE SKELETON OF A BIRD
caught last year in the hedge
winnows wind
and smoke. Between the white

Wall the fire
burns low, water still oozes
from soft mushrooms. A dog's still
circling in the juniper to make,

with belly and flanks, its bed.
Nearby, lying tossed away,
in the pond silt,
the hard nest, the sign.

Slowly, it grows soaking up
the water from below: the clumsy
wingless larva, between the white wall
and white feather,

Where the fire burns low.

NEDOUSUŠÍ SE HOUSLAŘ
střívek, otče, za tmy odchází
a za světla se nenavrací. Sotva
ho kdy potkám, i

Kdybych s každou v botách
spal, i kdybych za ním na páteř
z ryby pískal. U nás
teď chladno, stromy

Smirkuje jinovatka, víno
a kouře, u nás, plazivé.
Sotva se letos ohřeju
pod nehtem štiplavého hroznu.

FATHER, THE VIOLINMAKER DOESN'T DRY
the cat gut, he goes out into the darkness
and won't return to the light again. I hardly
ever meet him, even

If I keep my shoes on in bed
each time I sleep with a woman, even if
I whistle at him on a fish spine. It's cold
here now. Hoar frost

Grinds the trees. Here, grapevines
and smoke, creeping.
This year I can hardy get warm
under the fingernail of the sour grape.

ŘÍDKÝ JE ŘÍJEN
a v celém domě jediný
rozeschlý džber. Čevotočivé
světlo pracuje,

Ze stromů píšťaly, a já
nidke. A pavouček zatím
sliní vlákno jako
kdyby už svítání...

Je. Je daleko
kamkoliv, je hluboko odevšad.
Bojím se přes dvůr,
tam skořápky a nať.

OCTOBER IS OBLIQUE
a lone leaky pail
in the entire house. Worm-eaten
light is working,

Trees turn to whistles, and me,
I'm nowhere. Meanwhile,
a little spider spits out thread as if
it were already dawn...

It is. It's far
no matter where you turn, so far.
I'm afraid of what's across the courtyard—
the empty nutshells and leaves out there.

VLHKÉ MYŠI SPÁNKU
a vyvátá srst ve spárách
prken, po novinách, v rozkroku
vápnem pohozených stěn.

Do ticha tichá
plíseň tenkými zvonky
zní. Ukládá se žena
vedle mne, veliká,

Omytá řepná hlava,
průvan zpod okenic
ji v očních důlcích
zhasíná svíci.

SLEEP'S DAMP MICE
and matted fur in the floorboard
cracks, along the newspapers, in the crotch
of the whitewash-spattered walls.

The silent mold sounds
its tenuous bell
into silence. A woman lies down
beside me, her head

A huge washed beetroot.
A draft from the windows
blows out a candle
in the sockets of her eyes.

POHÁDKA O MNĚ. POD HABREM
kozlíka přistrojili. Nozdry
mu moukou leštím,
ženich a rekrut, a sama

Nevěsta hřebelec má a víno.
Růži za uchem já, růži
za uchem on. Poprvé
se ohlédnu, krocan křídly tluče,

Podruhé se ohlédnu, nevěsta
na kameni drží hádka,
a on slepýš. Potřetí
se vrátím, tentokrát nadosmrti.

Umřu.

A FAIRYTALE ABOUT ME. UNDER THE IRONWOOD
they've hitched up a billy goat. I polish
up his nostrils with flour, me,
the groom and recruit, and the bride, she's

Holding a comb and a sprig of grapevine.
A rose behind my ear, the goat has one
behind his. The first time
I look back, a turkey cock beats his wings,

The second time I look, the bride's
on a rock holding a small snake
and he's got a blindworm. The third time,
I'll come back, this time forever.

I'll die.

NA LÍSKÁCH VZLÍNÁ POPEL
jablečných odkrojků, krájených
ještě mými prsty, ronícími,
tehdy borůvkovou krev. Ze

Starých pytlů na půdě
vyvěrá pramínek zrní. Lísky
se potáhly srstí a světlem
z vikýře. Cítím se mužem.

Pouštím po jazyku víno, slavnostně
se opíjím, vždyť dole,
v modré světnici, pod prachem,
draným v podvečerech,

Vychází z moučných stehen
mé ženy: syn, voňavý
a trpký jako suchá jablka
a mokrý jíl.

ON THE CRATES, THE RESIDUE
of the apple parings cut
by my fingers still dripping with the blood
of the blueberries back then. A stream

of grain springs from an old sack
in the attic. The crates
are covered with tufts of animal hair and light
from the dormer. I feel like a man.

I let the wine run down my tongue. I get
festively drunk because downstairs
in the blue sitting room, in early evening,
beneath the down quilt,

My son comes out from between
my wife's floury thighs, smelling sweet
and bitter like dried apples
and damp earth.

V RYBNIČNÉM BAHNU
studený kmen, na kterém, ještě
postřísněni ranním popelem,
sedíš. Pařáty racků

Derou dno. Rukopis hladiny
svinuje vítr, je to jiná řeč,
pouze slova se nemění.
O skřele lína, do půli

Pohřbeného v bahně,
zachytil se list. Je
po výlovech, osychá
voda, třepí se síť. Je

Pozdě. Řeč stejná, pouze
slova se mění. Namísto včely,
která v létě zůstala ve vlasech,
vyčešeš matný, svraskalý smotek

S nesrozumitelným vzkazem.

THE COLD STUMP YOU SIT ON
in the pond mud,
while we're still dusted
with morning's ashes. The seagull's claws

Scrape bottom. The wind rolls up
the surface's manuscript, it's a different language,
only the words haven't changed.
A leaf gets caught

In the gills of a carp half-buried
in the mud. The fishing
is done. The water dries
out. The net's frayed. It's

Late. The same language, only
the words have changed. Instead of the bee
that got caught in your hair last summer,
you comb out the matted, shriveled tangle

With its unintelligible message.

JE DALEKO KAMKOLIV,
obloha nízská, nad
stropen strop. Daleká
na dotek, ty,

Obkroužená ještě slanou
třtinou léta. Prcháš,
ale v tvém erbu
jenom třmen. Skřitkové

Tvoji odrostli myším
pelíškům. Už nejsou tví,
u nás, s dveřmi, pod
které sněží třtina léta.

IT'S FAR NO MATTER WHERE YOU TURN,
a low sky, a ceiling
above the ceiling. Far
beyond reach, you,

Surrounded by the still salty
marsh reeds of summer. You run
but there's only a yoke
on your coat of arms. Your goblins

Have outgrown their mouse
holes. They're no longer yours,
the marsh reeds snow in
from under door at our place.

PO HROZNECH
jenom vinný kámen, po loužích
s hastrmánky opilců a žabkou-
královnou, nezůstal ani

Kruh, do něhož není radno
vstoupit. Jen sucho, nedotknuté
rozličnými dešti, čeká,
kdo požene ulicí,

Dehtem a peřím pomazané.
Tak u nás. Tak není o čem
s tebou spát, o chlebu, o vodě,
o krátkých bičících na kůži břicha

AFTER THE GRAPES
only the sediment, after the puddles
with the drunkards' water goblins and the frog-
queen, there wasn't even

A circle left that you shouldn't
set foot in. Only the drought untouched
by the bouts of rain waits
for someone to chase it,

Tarred and feathered through the streets.
That's how it is here. So it's not about
sleeping with you, about bread, about water,
about the quick pulses of sperm on the skin of
    your belly.

ŽÍLA RYBNÍKA, OBROSTLÁ
měkkým sádlem, mechem
a slizkou korou, sotva
se plazí. Pod

Rentgenovým světlem
vane kost, dnes
už lehounká, svátá
k rákosí. Zalžu—

Nezalžu, musím
to říci, navždy,
dokud pod jazykem
kvete řeč.

THE POND'S VEIN, COATED
with soft fat, moss
and scum, barely
creeps. Under

the x-ray's light
a bone blows. Now
light as a feather, it blows
towards the reeds. I'll tell lies—

I won't. I must
speak forever
for as long the words bloom
under my tongue.

RÁNO JEŠTĚ TMA,
slůj lesa, mokré přesličky,
štěpí se zpátky z uhlí
noci. Vidím: od stromu

Ke stromu vlkodlak
se zelenou loučí. Orosený
pavouk, můj otec. Ztrácí se,
avšak kudy a kde.

V pavučinách. Tak cestou
vycházíme, je slunce. Avšak vidím:
od otce se neodklopil stín.

MORNING STILL DARK,
a forest grotto, the damp horsetail,
splits back into the coal
of night. I see: moving from tree

To tree, a werewolf
with green kindling. A dewy
spider, my father. He's become lost,
but whither and where?

In spider webs. The path
leads us out, it's
sunny. But I see:
the shadow hasn't lifted from my father.

ŠUPINA LÍNA NA DNĚ
lejty, pozdvihované za mlh
k rybímu prstenci,
trvá. Suchý sníh

Kolnou protahuje. Zvedá se
chomáč psích chlupů,
pergamen netopýra
vraská. Sypu sůl,

do nízkých ohňů, listopadovou
sypu sůl. Modré
žilky ohně se zvolna
otvírají, prohoří—

vají součky suků.
Mám naspěch, šupino,
každý den dorostou
nehty, které zatneš.

THE SCALE ON THE BOTTOM
of the barrel, lifted out of the murk
towards the circle of fish,
remains. Dry snow

Blankets the shed. A tuft
of dog hair rises,
the bat's parchment
shrivels. I pour salt,

On the low-burning fires, I pour
November's salt. The fire's
blue veins slowly
open, burn-

ing through the gnarled bark.
Scale, I'm in a hurry.
The nails you'll use to grab
me are growing longer every day.

KŘIK BAŽANTA,
dávivý, zase jindy v krátkém
slunci. Otec se smeká
za ním po listí,

Které odsává zemi olej,
kronikář tohoto stěhovavého
měsíce, s naběhlým
hřebínkem, kohout

Na šípkových plotech. Je
pozdě, u nás, má žena
to ví, už jenom pýcha
mne nutí hledat znak

Pro sykot dřeva vzníceného
deštěm, křik bažanta
a kámen, který se, než
usnu, převaluje ve zdi.

THE CRY OF THE PHEASANT,
at another time in the waning
sunlight. My father goes after
it, slipping across the leaves,

That sap the earth of its oil,
the chronicler of the errant
moon, a cock
with a swollen comb

On the sweetbriar fence. It's
late at our place, my wife
knows, it's only pride
that forces me to seek the sign

For the hiss of the wood ignited
by rain, the cry of the pheasant
and the rock that's rolling
in the wall before I fall asleep.

VYSOKÉ BLÁTO,
obrácené tankem, snímá podobu
krajiny, tady. Při cestě,
nízké švestky, vyvrácené

Posledním škubem šlahounů,
s travou splétají se. V
těsnopisu suché révy
na zdi hospody:

Tvrdé hnízdo, znak. Daleká
bláta snímají posmrtnou
masku léta. Slyším:
táhne blátem, oštěkáván psy,

Pilňak. Ženské oplzle
pozpěvují při vytínání
zelných hlávek. Bosý
jde, Boris, obrýlený Rus.

THE DEEP MUD,
flipped over by a tank, makes a cast
of the countryside, here. En route,
the low-lying plums, torn away

By a final tug on the branches,
get mixed in with the grass. In
the withered vine's shorthand
on the wall of the pub:

A hard nest, the sign. The far away
patches of mud cast the death
mask of summer. I hear:
Pilnyak,* wading through the mud,

Dogs barking at him. Women bawdily
croon as they lop cabbage heads
in two. Walking around barefoot,
Boris, the bespectacled Russian.

---

* Boris Pilnyak (1894–1938). A Russian writer critical of Soviet society. He
was sentenced to death and executed after being tried for treason for
supposedly providing French writer André Gide with material for his
influential and scathing 1936 exposé about the Soviet Union, *Return from
the USSR*.

KRAJINA S ERBEM

COUNTRY WITH
A COAT OF ARMS

Pozůstalí

Svět se oteplí
a mrtví vypučí a vzkvetou.
—PAUL CELAN

1
a vršil se déšť a hlína, srpnové trombóny
už klestily se říjnem,
u zídky keř

2
a já opodál, pozůstalý,
po duběnkách, po inkoustu,
po vápnu a po přeslici,

3
s lýtky obrůstajícími keřem,
s očima puklýma jak kaštan,
nádherně živý v čepici,

4
a čepice je drn,
sopečná čapka v krajině řípů,
kde čenichá déšť a vrší se hlína

Survivors

*It's growing warm in the world
and the dead burgeon and bloom*
—PAUL CELAN

1
and the rain and earth piled up, august's trombones
already pruned back by october
a bush by a small wall

2
and me, nearby the survivor,
after the oak galls, ink,
whitewash and womankind,

3
my calves covered over by a bush,
my eyes bulging like chestnuts,
delightfully alive in my cap,

4
and the cap is made of sod,
a volcanic cap in the land of dormant volcanoes,
where the rain sniffs around and the earth piles up

5
i nad námi,
hraju na housle drnem, usmířen
s mrtvým, který se proto již nikdy—

6
neusmíří se mnou,
i když zvon se kýve v kloubech
a v jamkách klíčních kostí—

7
stojí pokojná voda,
zatímco kamery vrčí
otloukej se zvone,

8
srnci prchají z trombónů a vítr
čechrá křídla kamenným holubicím,
zatímco mrtvý roste před očima,

9
neboť ještě lpí na živých, chce
se jim ukázat, bují
a prostírá se jako houba,

10
nestačili ho poučit, jak se pokorně
obracet v prach, jak trpělivě
rozmlouvat s hluchoněmými anděly,

5
even above us,
i play the violin with sod, at peace
with the dead man who will never

6
make his peace with me,
even though a bell swings in his joints
and the pits of his collarbone—

7
the water stands still
as the news cameras whir,
clang away, bell,

8
deer run from the trombones and the wind
rustles the wings of a stone dove,
while, before my eyes, the dead man grows,

9
because he still clings to the living, he wants
to show them, he burgeons
and swells like a mushroom,

10
teaching him how to wallow humbly
in the dust wasn't enough for them to patiently
commune with deaf angels,

11
ještě lpí spíše na živých, ale již
se nemůže rozpomenout,
nikdy se nepřikrýval vlajkou,

12
věnce ho škrtí, nezvykl dosud
svému kousku pevniny,
která vláčena deštěm,

13
uplouvá nezadržitelně jinam,
dříve než se pozůstalí stačí rozejít
na svůj kousek pevniny,

14
dříve než se obě
navzájem
začnou vychylovat jako váhy,

15
nyní a zde, pod zvonem rozkývaným
jen vlaštovčím křídlem,
nechávaje mne opodál, obrůstat,

16
keřem, pozůstalého s očima
puklýma jak kaštan,
nádherně živého v čepici,

11
he still prefers to cling to the living, but
he can't remember anymore,
he never wrapped himself in a flag,

12
garlands strangle him, since he's no longer
accustomed to his patch of earth
hauled around by the rain,

13
it sails unstoppably elsewhere
before the survivors manage to scatter
to their own patches of earth,

14
before both
in unison
start to seesaw like scales,

15
here and now, beneath a bell set swaying
by the mere touch of a swallow's wing
leaving me nearby, to get overgrown

16
by the bush, the survivor with eyes
bulging like chestnuts,
delightfully alive in his cap,

17
a čepice je drn

27.8.1968

17
and the cap is made of sod

8.27.1968

Kámen v září
(fragment)

Cesta vzhůru je cestou dolů
—HERAKLEITOS

Čas minulý a budoucí čas, to,
co se mohlo stát, a co se stalo,
směřuje k jedinému cíli,
jenž je vždycky přitomný.
—T.S. ELIOT

I.
JSEM
znovu v Moorově krajině,
ve vřesech,
které hoří pokojně a modře
jako líh,
v kamení
a v bezvětrných vřesech tvých
kámen světlo,
kámen kámen,
kámen sůl,
v krajině bez hnízd, kde ptáci
nad perořízkem dálnice,
nad ovcí, která tu pokojně
a modře krvácí...

nepřezimují.

A Rock in September
(fragments)

The way up and the way down are one and the same
—HERACLITUS

Time present and time past...
What might have been and what has been
Point to one end, which is always present.
—T.S. ELIOT

I.
I AM
in the country Henry Moore once again
in the briar
that burns peaceful and blue
as hard liquor,
in the rocks
and your calm briars,
rock light,
rock rock,
rock salt,
in a country without nests, where the birds
above the letter opener of the road,
above a sheep here who bleeds gentle
and blue...

won't fly south for the winter.

ll.
tříští se kost
shledávám úlomky
v nemotorné bezkřidlé
larvě mé krajiny
snímané blátem

mezi vykloubenými stromy
mezi doutnajícími stromy
mezi ukřižovanými stromy
mezi drátěnými stromy
mezi ochraptělými stromy
mezi stromy a stromy které
dáví kost vlastního stínu
pavle

(z korespondence)

11.
a bone shatters
I pick up the pieces
in the inert, wingless
larva of my country
in the shorthand of my country
cast in mud

among the disjointed trees
among the smoldering trees
among the crucified trees
among the wiry trees
among the hoarse trees
among trees and trees that
choke on the bone of their own shadows,
pavel

(from correspondence)

III.
CO PEŘÍ MÁ,
všechno lítá. Netopýr,
anděl vyhnaný z křoví,
a tlustá husa peřiny. Veronika,
solný kamínek,
se směje, tříští
zlaté zmrazky,
její ruce
v mé rukavici. Z rukavice
prsty rozběhly se.
Poletují, do sněhu zobou.
Sníh lítá, peří má.
Hrajeme:
co nohy má, všechno padá...

Sníh se popelí

III.
THOSE WITH FEATHERS
all fly together. The bat,
the angel banished from the brush,
and the fat goose of the featherbed. Veronika,
the salty pebble,
smiles, shatters
the golden patches of ice,
her hands
in my glove. Released,
her fingers fly in all directions.
They take off, peck at the snow.
The snow flies, its feathers glide.
We're playing:
those with legs all must finally fall...

The snow wallows in ashes.

IV.
mávám srpnovou větví
až ruka usychá
hrajeme:
král vysílá své vojsko—
sám poručík Apollinaire
huláká z fáče:
udeřme na ně z boku
bim bam bum pif paf puf

mávám zelenou větví
až piliny z ní víří
divoce luskám prsty
až poletují kolem
jako hobliny
jen palec si ponechávám:
1) na památku
2) k ucpání klíčové dírky
3) Veronice na hraní
4) pro otisk

IV.
I wave August's branch
until my hand's dry
we play:
the king summons his troops—
Lonely Lieutenant Apollinaire
bellows through gauze bandages:
let's strike them from the flank
bim bam boom pif paf poof

I wave a green branch
until the sawdust swirls
savagely I snap my fingers
until they fly about
like wood chips
my thumb's all I'll keep:
1) for remembrance's sake
2) for plugging up keyholes
3) for Veronika to play with
4) for its print

V.
ROZSTÍNĚNÝ OBRAZ—
Moorovy krajiny. Stojí tam,
pod obnaženým nebem,
čistá jako vejce,
socha ženy.
Vzepjatá na patách,
tam, někde...
odkud a kam
je stejně daleko,
rameny zvedá svah
a loktem hloubí
rokli.

Zářijové světlo
vzdouvá obzor,
kane vosk.

Napjatá kůže vzduchu.
Kámen dne
padá.
Kámen dna.

(Tvrdili mi v básních, že samota,
která není z lidí...
je obývána anděly.)

Silnice, vyťatá
v ohništi vřesu.
Kane vosk.

V.
A CHIAROSCURO LANDSCAPE—
Moore's country. Standing there,
under heaven laid bare,
a statue of a woman,
inviolate as an egg.
Arching backwards
there, somewhere...
whence and where
are equally far,
with her shoulders, she lifts the hillside
with her elbow, hollows out
a gorge.

September's light
makes the horizon swell,
wax drips.

The air's taut skin
Day's rock
drops.
Rock-bottom rock.

(They told me in poems the solitude,
not of humankind...
is inhabited by angels.)

The road, dead-ended
in a firepit of briar.
Wax drips.

Tiše vzlíná
až k čáře,
kde voda oblohy
už opadává.
Solný kamínek,
má dcera, spí,
se spícími vlasy,
průhledná
na úpatí září
jako svazek cibule
na příčlích
dešťového altánu...

Můj rozstíněný obraz
světelné Moorovy krajiny.

Quietly it rises
to the line
where the sky's water
has already fallen.
The salty pebble,
my daughter, sleeps
with sleepy hair,
transparent
on September's foothill
like a bunch of onions
on the beams
of a rain-drenched arbor....

My chiaroscuro landscape
of Moore's luminous country.

VI.
ukazují na mne prstem
lákají do hry
berou mne za prst do kola
za nos za uši za vlasy
za flígr do kola:

pec nám spadla pec nám spadla
čum na sebe do zrcadla
ať je to ten nebo ten
nastehuje stejný sten
pec nám spadla pec nám spadla
čum na sebe do zrcadla
teď jsi myš a teď jsi pták
nebo klidně naopak

VI.
they point their fingers at me
they tempt me to play
grab me by the finger to make me take my turn
by the nose ears hair
scruff of the neck one after the other:

patty cake patty cake baker's man
look in the mirror if you can
eeny meeny miny moe
catch a tiger make him groan
patty cake patty cake baker's man
look in the mirror if you can
now you're a mouse and now a bird
or easily the reverse

VII.
PŘED SKOTSKEM, ZA SKOTSKEM,
začínám s Veronikou hru.
Její čtyři léta v zemi
plyšových koníků
a mých osmadvacet
v dosud bezejmenné
ulici dosud bezejmenného města,
přibližují jí vše,
co se vzdaluje,

jako mně vzdalují,
co se přibližuje.
Slova jí stoupají
z mléčného hrdla
jako sníh. Není hran,
vše zaobleno.
Blízkost i vzdálenost
se protínají v uzlu,
který jí později
pojmenují láskou.

Zatíim tiskne
na zápraží housátko
se stejnou oddaností,
s jakou mu o chvíli později
vystrojí na zahradě pohřeb.

VII.
ONE SCOTCH, TWO SCOTCH, THREE SCOTCH,
     FOUR,
I start a game with Veronika.
Her four years in the land
of toy ponies
and my twenty-eight
on a heretofore unnamed street
of a heretofore unnamed city,
Everything that retreats
comes near her

the way everything that comes near
retreats from me.
Words rise
from her milky throat
like snow. There's no hard edge,
all is curved.
Proximity and distance
intersect at the node
they'll later tell her
is called love.

Meanwhile on the porch
she'll choke the gosling
with the same devotion,
that a moment later in the garden,
she'll use to perform its funeral.

Zatím je stejně lítostná
nad ohryzanou kůrou stromku
jako nad hladem zdivočelým králíkem.
Není hran, vše zaobleno,

jako sníh stoupají slova
z mléčného hrdla
v zemi plyšových koníků
a živých
i mrtvých housat.

Meanwhile, she'll feel the same regret
for the gnawed bark of a sapling
that she does for the wild rabbit's hunger.
There's no hard edge, all is curved,

like snow, words rise
from her milky throat
in the land of toy ponies
and goslings
alive and dead.

VIII.
jenže z oblohy
je nedosypáno kamene
v mé krajině s erbem
jímž tvrdé hnízdo
znak
je nedosypáno kamene
nad šumícím borem
nad ochraptělým stromem
nad stromy s vyříznutým srdcem
ty mlčící
nad stromy s vyříznutým jazykem
ty křičící
nad stromy které
polykají kost vlastního stínu
pavle
(z úst do kůže)

Vlll.
but there are rocks
still to fall from the sky
in my country with a coat of arms
the hard nest
the sign
is the rocks still to fall
on the rustling grove
on the hoarse tree
on the trees with their hearts cut out
the ones that keep silent
on the trees with their tongues cut out
the ones that scream
above the trees that
swallow the bone of their own shadows
pavel
(from mouth to skin)

IX.
ČAS MINULÝ
a budoucí čas, to, co se mohlo stát
a co se stalo, směřuje
k jedinému cíli,
jenž je vždycky přitomný.
V kruhu se vracím.

Po osmadvaceti letech mezi
spolužáky, knihami,
ženou, spolucestujícími,
spolužijícími a zpolamrtvými
mám dceru. O chvíli později
otočí kruh ženu,
z níž se život
bude odštěpovat
ve vrstvách,
v dětech,
v listech:
průhledných a matných
jako slída.

Blízkost a vzdálenost
se protnou v uzlu,
který jí jeden nazve zákonem
a druhý usmířením.

IX.
THE PAST TENSE
and future, what might have been
and what has, aims
towards a single goal
that's ever present.
I come full circle.

After twenty-eight years, among
classmates, books,
wife, traveling companions,
life companions and those half-dead.
I have a daughter. A moment later
the circle turns, a woman,
from whom life
will be stripped away
in layers,
in children,
in sheets of paper:
transparent and opaque
like mica.

Proximity and distance
converge in a nexus
someone tells her is law
and someone else reconciliation.

X.
nemel nemel vylož
karty na stůl
rozpárejte mu rukávy
popište mi ho:
tváří se mrtvým?
nebo živým?
roste mu na dlani chlup?
jaké barvy?
zúčastnil se školního výletu?
na říp?
před skotsko za skotsko?
o jaké soše to hovoří?
věří v kobylí vejce?
je zklamán že nevěří?
pronesl protokolovanou nemravnost
ukázala cecek/
kropenatý všecek/
co krupička to rok/
a co čech to prorok/?
jestli ano komu a v kolik hodin?
co o tom soudí dnes?
soudí někdy něco o něčem?
jestli ano z čeho tak usuzuje?
pučí mu snad uši jako květáky?
hlava jako dýně?
ohanbí jako mech?
atd?
kde?
nebo kudy?

X.

don't bluff don't bluff lay
your cards on the table
rip apart his sleeves
describe him to me:
is he playing dead?
or alive?
is there hair growing on his palm?
what color?
did he go on the school field trip?
to říp?
one scotch, two scotch, three scotch, four?
what statue is he talking about?
does he buy that tale about the mare hatched from an egg?
is he disappointed that he doesn't?
did he smuggle out the documented depravity?
did it flash its tits/
its mottled bits/
a birthmark appearing every year/
and every Czech a soothsayer/?
if so whose fortune and at what hour?
what's he make of it today?
does he ever think anything about something?
if so what's the reason why?
maybe his ears will swell like cauliflowers?
his head like a pumpkin?
his genitals like moss?
and so on?
where?
or whither?

XI.
NYNÍ A ZDE A ZNOVU
pod obnaženým nebem,
v Moorově krajině
se sochou ženy
s ústy rozbolavělými
skelnými chloupky broskví.
A nikdy právě jen nyní
a nikde právě jen zde.
V kruhu.

Cesta vzhůru je cestou dolů
a já návratech
zas jednou nohou na útěku.
Pomalý střípek koluje v krvi
Moorovy sochy.
Kámen let padá.
Kámen letu.

Slova se mění, stejná řeč.
Nacházíme jen to, s čím se míjíme.
Poblíž a nikdy blízko.
Umíme promlouvat jen mlčením.
Jsem vyzáblý a vrhám kyprý stín
Daleko, ale nikdy vzdálen.
Umím se hájit jen vlastní obžalobou.
Kámen dne padá.
Kámen dna.

XI.
HERE AND NOW AND AGAIN
under the sky laid bare,
in Moore's country,
with a statue of a woman
her lips aching
from glassy peach fuzz.
And never right now
and nowhere right here.
In the circle.

The way up and the way down are one and the same
and I'm returning
again with one foot out the door.
The slow splinter goes round and round in the blood
of Moore's sculpture.
The years' rock falls.
The rock in flight.

The words change, the language stays the same.
We find only that which makes us slip away.
Nearby and never near.
We can speak up only by shutting our mouths.
I'm skin and bones and I cast a fleshy shadow.
Far, but never far off.
I can plead my case only with my very own indictment.
Day's rock drops.

The rock of rock bottom.

z

BROŽOVANÉ
BÁSNĚ

from
PAPERBOUND
POEMS

Zrození básníka: preambule

Bude maso bude křen
Už se klubeš opeřen
Už ti hochu pleny žehlí
Brkem vízneš v břichu jehly
Už ti šijí rubášek
Házej stěnu na hrášek
Zpátky nelze: musíš ven

Jonáš z jícnu vyvržen

The Poet's Birth: Preamble

There'll be meat, there'll be fish
You're pecking at the other chicks
Boy, they have your nappies ready
See the pins stuck at your belly
They're sewing you a winding sheet
Throw your pearls at the swine's feet
You can't turn back: you must go on

Jonah belched out of Leviathan

Konec básníka: preambule

Měřil jsem o dvě hlavy víc než Stalin
Obě dvě hlavy plné mýtů
A ze svých neprůhledných vnitřních krajin
Pouštěl jsem hejna kuřat v igelitu:

Své verše tehdejší

Už mám jen jednu hlavu a páteř se mi sesedá
Držím se při zemi a žiji vesměs ze zvyku
A do svých otevřených vnitřních krajin vodím souseda
Na transparentní kuře v aspiku:

Své verše vezdejší

The Poet's End: Preamble

Once I was two heads taller than Stalin
Chock-full of myth both of them were
I shooed away the flocks of frozen hens
Out of the dark reaches of my interior:

My verses back in the day

Now I've just one head and sagging ass
I've my feet on the ground and I live by habit
I show my neighbor around my inner expanse
To the filmy chicken set there in aspic:

My verses today

Lán

(Václavu Havlovi)

...Třebaže hável je prý
Hebrejsky marnost
A ty se hrozíš lepry
Rýmů
A lyrického chřípí...

Právě ty lyrik jsi!

...V brumendu apokalypsy
Vystoupiv z chóru
Sám jako babka jednotící
Lán krmné české řípy
Jdeš...

Lyrická tečko na obzoru!

Lea

(For Václav Havel)

Though Havel I'm told
Is the Hebrew for vanity
And you loathe
Lepers of rhyme
And lyric noses...

That's just what you are, a lyric poet!

...Taking leave of the choir
In the apocalypse's din
Like the crone in the lea
Thinning rows of beets
You go it alone...

The lyric full stop on the horizon!

Cesta do Ďáblic

(Josefu Kroutvorovi)

Leb lysá jak misál
A uvnitř jsi sám
Sám ve svém ghettu
Třebaže před tebou tu jsou a byli jiní

Faust který našeptával Goethu
Tě nikdy neobviní
Že se mu z bázně vyhýbáš
Když v noci jezdíš do Ďáblic
A sobě na kuráž
Zkoušíš si zahvízdat:

To strach odvaze diktuje
Svůj samizdat

The Road to Ďáblice

(For Josef Kroutvor)

Bald as the prayer book
You live in alone
Alone in your ghetto
Where before you others lived.

Faust who used to whisper in Goethe's ear
Wouldn't call it a sin
If you avoid him like the plague
when you go to Ďáblice ** at night
And whistle to yourself
to get your mettle back:

Fear dictates to courage
Its samizdat

---

* **Josef Kroutvor (1942).** Art historian, distinctive philosopher, and theorist
of the poetic school of Czech slapstick. He published only in *sazmizdat*.

** **Ďáblice.** A section in north Prague that could be translated *at the place
of she-devils*

81

Prostřední ze sester Brontëových píše dopis

(Rudolfu Matysovi)

Příteli básníku!

Ne nesahejte na kliku
U mocných hodinářů srdce
Snažně Vás prosím můj milý
Nechte si staré šelesty
Svá slova...šero...styl...
Své srdce s překlepy i omyly
A denně poduste je na cibulce

Tak jako na Větrné hůrce

Vaše oddaná Emily

The Middle Brontë Sister Writes a Letter

(For Rudolf Matys)[*]

Friend Poet!

Don't touch the movement
On the great clockmaker's heart
My dear friend please
Hang on to your past scribbling
Your words... darkness... style
Your heart's blunders and inaccuracy
Sauté them daily and make a stew

The way at Wuthering Heights they do

Your devoted Emily

---

[*] **Rudolf Matys (1938).** Poet, literary critic, and essayist.

Básník

(Oldřichu Mikuláškovi)

Má v lenním právu ulici
Holí je proklepává
A v chůzi zkouší číst
Dno z kruhů na hladině
Učí se ze rtů odezírat plynně
O čem a kterak město mlčí
S podzimním stínem na plicích
Má v lenním právu ulici
A ví když vbíhá autům pod kola
Že smrt města je lidská:
Čti k neupití pomalá...

84

Poet

*(For Oldrich Mikulášek)**

He's got feudal rights to a street
He taps at with a cane
As he walks he tries to read
Its depth by surface rings
He learned to read the city's lips
To know why it holds its tongue
And has dark spots on its lungs
He's got feudal rights to the street
And when the cars strike him
He gets the city's death is human:
That is—a slow binge that never ends...

---

* Oldrich Mikulášek (1910–1985). One of the most prominent Czech poets
of the late twentieth century, the author of great love poetry and reflec-
tive verse. He was the editor of the influential literary review *Host*. After
1969, he work appeared only unofficially in samizdat until 1980. In 1967,
he was struck by a car and severly injured. He used to walk around Brno
on crutches.

Causa mortalis

(Jiřímu Pištorovi in memoriam)

Sám se sebou v divoké tiché hádce
Jsi pochopil že nikdy nikomu s ničím
Skutečně svým se nesvěříš
Nýbrž sám sebe pozorovat budeš jak za tebou
Poušť a nádherné duny přivátého písku
Před tebou případně naopak
Sám se sebou v divokém tichém smíření
Napůl ryba a napůl pták
Vzlétl jsi k nejhlubšímu prameni

Causa Mortalis

(In memory of Jiří Pištora)[*]

Wildly and silently arguing with yourself
You realized you'd never trust anything
Of your own to someone else
Instead you regard what's behind you
The desert's exquisite windblown dunes
While before you it's the reverse
Once you wildly and silently made your peace
Part fish part bird
You flew away to the deep dark spring

---

[*] Jiří Pištora (1932–1970). A poet, essayist, and literary critic whose early life was marked by the tragic event of his father's execution by the Nazis for participating in Reinhard Heydrich's assassination. In his poetic work, Pištora explored themes of the loneliness, emptiness, and uncertainty of the human condition. After the Soviet Invasion in 1968 and the social and political ruin that followed during normalization, Pištora felt that his only recourse, in a world bereft of hope, was to take his own life.

Pražský žalm

(Karlu Šiktancovi)

Do javorových desek ukládáš své tisky
A já se bojím že mne stihne boží hněv
Za svatokrádež plisky
Kterou jsi míval ve své ředitelně…
Zatím zapřený strýček undergroundu
Stal se ze mne a věřím na Strom poznání
Třebaže ňák den po dni od kořenů hnije
A před očima usychá mi tolik jeho kmínků
Ach bratře v rýmu! Zachrání při Posledním soudu
Opilé nehodné ovečky nebeská amnestie
A smyje jejich krákoravou hanbu
Či aspoň sleví na podmínku
Když řeknou: "Já jsem někdo jiný?"?
A my? Žalobu stáhne náš vesnický pánbů
A vyhostí nás do pražštiny?!

A Prayer for Prague

(For Karel Šiktanc)[*]

You set the type in trays of maple
And I fear the gods' wrath
For pinching the tipple
You used to stash in your desk...
The incognito uncle of the underground they've made
    meantime
Of me and I still have faith in Eden's tree though
Its roots have withered and died every day before my
    eyes
Oh brother in rhyme!
Will the worthless drunken lambs be spared on
    Judgment Day
Will they regain their purity
Or at least be granted amnesty
When they say like Rimbaud, "I is another"?
And will our village's demigod then mercifully
Exile us to Prague's vernacular?

---

[*] **Karel Šiktanc (1928).** Poet, editor, and former Managing Editor at Mladá Fronta Publishing House, the publisher of Šrut's collection *Worm-Eaten Light* in 1969. Shortly after the book's publication, Šiktanc was fired from his position. From 1969 to 1989, he could only publish officially in samizdat at home, and abroad, in editions by Czech publishing houses in exile.

Epitaf

(sobě)

Zde leží ten
Co neužil pozemských statků
A nepřelez svůj vlastní plot
Zato však rád do zadku
Kopal se párem cizích bot

Bylo to tak a nejináč:
On prázdnou slámu mlátil
U šenku kvetl zavináč
A rum mu život zkrátil

Epitaph

(For Me)

Here lies the man
Who didn't make use of his worldly goods
Or try to climb across his fence
Wearing someone else's shoes
He liked to kick himself instead

That's just the way it had been:
He threshed the grain's empty hulls
The peanuts at the bar beckoned
He cut short his life drinking rum

Houpací Trojský kůň I.

Dokud jsem nebydlel v tom Trojském koni
Jaksi jsem držel se víc v pořádku
Rýmy jsem si dal platit od řádku
A nesmrkal jsem mezi prsty případně do rukávu

Abych tak řekl: ztratil jsem se v davu
A bylo mně jak jemu
Oj trochu dobře trochu zle!
Dokud jsem nebydlel v tom Trojském koni

Neměl jsem tělo kostibásní prolezlé
Svá slova na jazyku jsem prostě polykal
Pro věčnou vzpomínku

A žádné trápení/plynatost/dluhy/kolika
Dokud jsem nebydlel v tom Trojskému koni
Uprostřed Prahy na rynku

Trojan Rocking Horse I.

Now that l live in the Trojan Horse
l feel so much more at ease
I've been paid by the line for my poetry
And don't wipe my nose on my sleeve

I've gotten lost in the crowd so to speak
Life's the same for the others as it is for me
A little better a little worse!
Now that l live in the Trojan Horse

My body's been chewed to the bone by verse
l simply swallow the words on my tongue
To preserve the memory eternally

And no worries/gas/debts/gripes
Now that l live in the Trojan Horse
In the center of Václavské náměstí

Kmotřička kocovina

Chodím městem a naslouchám mu očima
Hledím mu do uší
Hmatám jeho pohledy
Čichám jeho smutné veselí
Chci o tom napsat a píšu
Pozdech ulic
A hle ulice se sbíhají:
Jsem čten!

Naslouchají mi oči
Hledí na mne uši
Ohmatávají mne pohledy
Čihají mé smutné veselí
Chutnají mou porci vzduchu
Chci o tom napsat a píšu
Po zdech svého podnájmu
A hle zdi se sbíhají:
Jsem tištěn!

The Fairy Godmother of Hangover

I walk around the city and listen in on it with my eyes
I peer into its ears
I touch its gazes
I sniff its sad gaiety
I want to write about it and I write
Across the street walls
And lo and behold the streets converge:
I've been read!

They listen in on me with their eyes
They peer into my ears
They grope me with their gazes
They sniff my sad gaiety
They taste my serving of air
I want to write about it and I write
Across my apartment walls
And lo and behold the walls converge:
I've been printed!

Stalinův pomník:
momentka z roku 1956

Žulový orel snesl se na sokl
De po dni
Bdí nad Prahou aby snad ani kamínek
Z té sochy v příštích distich nezmokl
A pod ním
Přkován k posteli
V městském špitále Na Františku
S rozklovanými játry tatínek
Pročítá mou žákovskou knížku

Stalin's Monument:
A Candid Snapshot from 1956

On the monument the granite eagle lands
Day after day
Above Prague it vigilantly defends
The statue from the slightest bit of damp
And down below a ways
At the city hospital today
With his liver pecked apart
And tied down to his bed
Dad peruses my report card

U odvodu

"Jste chlapík!" řekli mi u odvodu
"Srdíčko máte jako Gagarin!"
Když v trenýrkách jsem vyběhl pár schodů

(Umělý med a margarin
Sice mi v dětství ubral sil
Rovnováhu však vyrovnal naštěstí rybí tuk)

"Ale on píše básně!" major utrousil
"Pero je taky zbraň!" rozhodl politruk
A neadresně povzdychl si: "Kokoti..."

(Dodneška vidím ho: byl droboučký a paťatý
Ale měl myšlenky které se snadno okotí—)

At My Induction into the Army

At my induction they cried, "You're a terrific chap!"
"Your heart's just like Gagarin's!"
They cheered when I ran a few steps

(Though the ersazt honey and margarine
Of my youth sapped my vitality
Fish oil balanced them out happily)

The Party Commissar proclaimed
"The pen's mightier than the sword!"
Then under his breath "you wanker" he quipped...

(I can see him even now: Lilliputian with a limp
But his ideas could breed as fast as rabbits)

Dechová cvičení

Inu jste kuřák ale rád se od plic zasmějete
Ovšem tím, že se zasmějete donutíte zároveň
Plíce ke kašli
Což vaši ženu tuze zarmucuje
Inu jste kuřák ale svou ženu milujete
Ovšem tím že ji milujete podléháte zároveň
Jejím zdravotním příkazům
Což vaši ženu tuze rozradostňuje
Inu jste kuřák ale provádíte pod jejím dohledem
Dechová cvičení
Ovšem tím provádíte míváte občas sny
V nichž vás vaše žena dusívá polštářem
Inu jste kuřák ale probouzíte se vždy neudušený
A svým snům se vždy rád od plic zasmějete

P.S.
Zkuste tuto báseň přečíst
na jedno nadechnutí

Deep Breathing Exercises

Sure you're a smoker still you enjoy a hearty laugh
Of course laughing causes you
To cough heartily as well
Which greatly upsets your wife
Sure you're a smoker still you love your wife
Of course since you love her
You give in to her edicts regarding your health as well
Which greatly delights her
Sure you're a smoker still under her watchful gaze
You do deep breathing exercises
Of course sometimes while you're doing them
You daydream that your wife's put a pillow over your
    face
Sure you're a smoker still you always wake up again
And in your dreams you always enjoy a hearty laugh

P.S.
Try reading this poem
In one breath

Dvojník

Kdepak mám asi dvojníka?
V Santa Fé? V Reykjaviku?
A zda místo mne utíká
Do sypkých kopců pro protěž
Jednoho totožného okamžiku?

Je-li sám na jednoho: na sebe
Proti tak strašné přesile
Tak jako já v tom čase rozdrobeném na chvíle

Kdopak se za nás oba zhostí
Údělu vlastní totožnosti?

My Double

Where oh where has my double gone?
To Santa Fe? To Saxe-Zeitz?
What if he's the one who's run
To the snowy peaks to pluck
A similar moment's edelweiss?

What if he's pitted against himself: friendless
All alone outnumbered and quite hopeless
As I am in this time that's shattered into moments

And who'll forgive us for the sin
Of being the other's identical twin?

Houpací Trojský kůň II.

Děti se houpají na Trojském koni
Děti se věčně ptají
Město je věčně plné praporů.
Děti se věčně ptají proč
Ale co asi se něco slaví říkáte a ony
Na povšechnou otázku žádají zcela určitou odpověď
Zcela určitě se něco slaví říkáte ale co to

Prapory zničehonic zmizí
Žerdě naprázdno skřípou
Děti poznají váš neklid
Poznají že jim něco tajíte
U večeře to skřípe
V noci vás skřípající postel
Obrací z boku na bok ale co to
Ráno je město plné praporů
A vy se ptáte proč
A děti vás houpají na Trojském koni.

Trojan Rocking Horse II.

The children rock on the Trojan Horse
The children always ask questions
The city is forever filled with flags
The children always ask why
But you say I guess they're celebrating something
    and they
Demand a definitive answer to this general question
So you say, they're definitely celebrating something,
    but what can you do

All of a sudden the flags disappear
The hollow flagpoles creak
The children can tell you're worried
They can tell you're hiding something from them
At dinner it creaks
At night your creaking bed
Tosses and turns you but what can you do
The next day the city's filled with flags
And you ask why
And the children rock you on the Trojan Horse.

Budoucnost

(Vítovi)

Čím dál víc se raduji
V hospodě mého srdce je čím dál víc hostí
Čím dál vic rozhovor mění se ve zmínky
O někom o něčem
A co se týče budoucnosti
Zapomínám i vzpomínky:

Vším co mne čeká
Netečně potěšen

The Future

(For Vit)

The more and more I have fun
More and more patrons come to my heart's pub
Their talk more and more turns to calumny
About someone or something
And whatever is to come
I forget even the memory:

All that awaits me
Rejoices passively

Adamova žena

Procitla vprostřed rajské zeleně
když had jí podal taj. přís. dův.
zprávu kde stálo cosi proti Adamovi

Z lásky a strachu z jistých míst
spálila téhož rána Adamův
fíkový list

(Obsahoval jen nečitelné poznámky
o počasí
a monogamní lásce

Plus školáckou studii jablka
s anatomickou kresbou ohryzku
kterou A.

z pochopitelných příčin nemínil
uvolnit ještě do tisku)

Adam's Wife

She'd awoke in the midst of Eden's greenery
when the snake offered her
the confidential file on Adam

Out of love and her fearful beliefs
that same day she burned
Adam's fig leaf

(It contained only unintelligible notes
about monogamous love
and the weather

Plus a schoolboy's study of an apple
With a sketch of an Adam's apple that was
    anatomically correct
Which A.
For obvious reasons didn't want
To make public yet)

Sisyfova žena

(Janovi a Božence Skácelovým)

Byl trochu naměkko jako by znal už trest
den před tím dnem kdy zprotivil se bohům
a jemný byl: kamínek vyklepal mi ze sandálu
a vymrštil jej prakem za oblohu
a vzpomínal jak s chlapci hrával drápky
a oblázky jak vytloukával z důlků
a jemný byl: nedbaje proudu ani lávky
z balvanu na balvan mne přenášel
a jinde kameny zas navršil a daroval mi most
a mluvil o čase a co když ten lidský dar ztratí
a já se hloupá ptala jaký dar
a on mi odpověděl: smrtelnost

Sisyphus's Wife

(For Jan and Boženka Skácel)[*]

He was close to tears as if he had known the penalty
the day before the day he angered the gods
and he was also gentle: from my sandal he dislodged
a pebble and shot it to heaven with a sling
and he remembered how as a child he went
out to play skittles and shoot glass marbles from the ring
and he was gentle: ignoring the footbridge and current
from boulder to boulder he carried me across
and piled up stones elsewhere to make a bridge for me
and he spoke of time and what if we'd lose our human gift
and me the fool asked *what* gift
and he answered: mortality.

---

[*] Jan Skácel (1922–1989). Poet, managing editor of the literary review *Host do domu*, and famous for his witty and poetic literary columns. From 1969 to 1981, Skácel could only publish in samizdat and abroad. His short poems, however, spread spontaneously among young people.

Démosthenova žena mluví v zlosti

Jó ten vám uměl držet jazyk
za zuby a zuby za rty
a raděj vlastní ukazovák
do vlastní řitě vstrčil by
než by jím ukázal na rub
té skvělé karty
kterou vždy bohům platíval
a tím získával úlitby

A řečnil tak že překřičel
i hukot moře v přílivu
zato však nikdy šelest mého šatu...
ten koktavec s ústy plnými oblázků
jenž sám nad sebou žasl
v němém obdivu
ten svislík můj a—promiňte mi rým—
mim plédující pro lásku!

Demosthenes's Wife's Diatribe

Oh he could be tight-lipped
and hold his tongue
and he'd rather stick
his own pointer up his bum
than reveal to them
the terrific trump
he used to pay the gods
for the libations that he'd drunk

And he orated so much he drowned out
the sea's roaring tide
but never those rustling skirts of mine...
a guy who stammers day and night
with marbles in his mouth
and a heart full of pride
my little hanger-on—please forgive the rhyme—
always begging for love that mime of mine!

Homérova žena si stýská

Co s mužem který čeká na odliv
aby se vydal brázdou Odyssea?
Co s ženou které se jenom příliv vrací?
(Když usínám jsem voliéra
unášejí mne uvnitř uvěznění ptáci)

Ne já si nestýskám
neříkám ještě včera...
A pláčem neslepnu
jako ten můj
když nad verši zrak ztrácí
a místo plachet má jen stůl

Ach nevěřte
on nikdy nevyplul

Homer's Wife's Lament

What can you do with the man who waits for low tide
to sail off in the wake of Odysseus?
And what can you do with a woman to whom only the
    high tide returns?
(I'm an aviary when I drift to sleep
I'm flown into the cage by the captive birds)

No, I'm not talking yesterday
I'm not going to bitch...
I won't go cry myself blind
like that husband of mine
with verse-ruined eyes
a man with a desk instead of a rudder

Oh, don't you believe him
he never weighed anchor

Galileova žena

Ze samé lásky raději zachová se podle
raději práskne dalekohled

Ne Galileo!

Sama sesmolí udání a s bázní přiloží
ten zrádný předmět doličný

Vždyť ten obcoval s Lunou
ten tryjédr ten falus
který k nebi ční...

Ne Galileo!

Což podepsat i před koncilem může
svou vlastní krví měsíční

Galileo's Wife

For love alone she'd rather be devious
she'd rather smash the telescope

Not Galileo!

Alone she cooks up the accusation
attaching the corpus delicti with trepidation

It consorted with Luna after all
the spyglass the phallus
jutting up to God

Not Galileo!

Something she'd even sign before the Tribunal
in her own menstrual blood

Že

Že tolikrát se divil volným veršem
že rybník opadává a zároveň kvete
že na břehu jeho čtyřiceti
ráno voní životem a večer smrdí smrtí

That

That so many times free verse had amazed him
that the pond blooms at the same time it ebbs
that now that he's on the brink of forty
morning smells sweet of life and night reeks of death

Dynastie Že

27. dubna kteréhosi roku vykouřil
43 cigaret vypil 7 piv a litr čaje
doslechl se o objevu nové hvězdy
v naší blízké galaxii vzpomněl si
na ústní koutek své dcery byl předvolán
do Bartolomějské k podání vysvětlení
zapamatoval si pětiverší anonyma
z dynastie Že napsal tuto báseň
se zamlčeným příběhem avšak nezamlčel

že 27. dubna k. r. vykouřil 43 cigaret
vypil 7 piv a litr čaje doslechl se
o objevu nové hvězdy a blízké galaxii Že
byl předvolán do Bartolomějské
k podání vysvětlení Že zapomněl pětiverší
anonyma z dynastie Že vzpomněl si
na vzdálený ústní koutek své dcery Že

The That Dynasty

on April 27th of some year he smoked
43 cigarettes drank 7 beers and a liter of tea
he heard about a new star's discovery
in a nearby galaxy he remembered
the corner of his daughter's mouth he was summoned
for an interrogation at Bartholomew St.*
he recalled the anonymous poet of classical *shi*
from the That Dynasty he wrote this poem
with the concealed meaning that didn't stay concealed

that on April 27th of said year he smoked 43 cigarettes
drank 7 beers and a liter of tea he
heard about a new star's discover in the nearby That
    Galaxy
that he was summoned to Bartholomew St.
for an interrogation So he forgot the anonymous poet
    of classical *shi*
from the That Dynasty that he
forgot the far off corner of his daughter's mouth That

---

* **Bartholomew St.** The location of the main interrogation headquarters of
  the StB, the Czech secret police, during the communist era.

V domácnosti

Kdybych se jak se říká
Též i já dostal k lizu
A u všech dveří klika
Byla by mé vízum
Nechal bych verše zaumné
Šukati po kuchyni
Kde ani stín mi neuhne
Ba tvrdí že já! stíním
A přerušil bych styky hned
S tzv. vnitřní emigrací
Jež beztak vízne: šutýrek
V hrdélku hodin přesýpacích!

Domestic Life

If I could ever win
A million dollar jackpot
Every door I'd open
Could be my passport out
I'd let my nonsense rhymes
Make chaos of my place
Where it never tries to hide
Why *I'm* the shadow it insists!
I'd sever all connection
To this so-called house arrest
Since in truth home's a prison:
Sand trapped in an hourglass!

Agent 007

Tak jsem ti koupil od známých lacino starší televizi
Aby ses nebála když večer ctnostně smolím rýmy
Jenomže obraz čas od času zmizí
A třetí program začne vysílat mé každodenní krimi
Honičky převleky přesmyčky podlézky tajenky
    zpronevěry
Zanedbávání cizích zevnějšků a vlastní dcery
Jakož i tebe a rovněž maminky a zdravé výživy a bratra
V tom Czech-bondovském seriálu nazvaném
Žijete jen dvakrát

Agent 007

I got you a cheap used TV from some people I know
So you wouldn't be afraid at night when I'm writing
   poems
But every now and then the picture goes
And Channel Three begins to air my crimes of the
   moment
The chases travesties puzzles petty faults and lack of
   common sense
Neglecting my daughter and my own appearance
This equally applies to mama my brother healthy
   living and you my wife
In this Czech James Bond serial they call
You only live twice

Kentaur

Nádherně jsem se probudil:
Vyskočím z postele a mám dva páry kopyt!

Odhodlán všeho starého
Nechat a všeho nového se chopit

Začínám orat vláčet sít a sklízet daktylem
Uznání čtená z očí Pegase:

V zrcadle podoben jsa kobyle
Poznávám se jen po hlase

Centaur

I woke up this morning feeling grand:
I jump out of bed on two sets of hooves!

I'm bent on leaving behind the old
To embrace everything new

I've started to plow harrow sew and reap with meter
The acknowledgment in the centaur's eyes I read:

In the mirror there's the form of a filly
Only by its voice can I tell that it's me

Domů

Jsem zralý muž a proto se rád vracím
Domů…po všech těch konspiracích
Jež denně podnikám
Po krčmách trafikách řeznících zelinářích
Odnikud do nikam
A pořád dokola a marně
Domů…ach domů kde se daří
Člověku žít alespoň trochu ilegálně!

Going Home

I'm a grown man and that's why I like to go
Home...after all those conspiracies
I undertake on a daily basis
After the dives, tobacco stores, butcher shops,
    and groceries
Going from nowhere to no place
Going forever in circles pointlessly
Going home...ah home where a man is still free
To live just the slightest bit illegally!

Ti dva

Co je k sobě poutá?

Právěže jen pouta
pasti slasti
tenata

Nevědí to
Ten a Ta

A Bůh?

Píše errata

The Two

What ties these two?

Truly only ties
of rapture's trap
the history of drudgery

They don't know it
He and She

And God?

He pens fallacy

Po dalším pohřbu

Oheň nás oddálil
a hlína nesblížila

Byl nebyl
Nežila žila

Mrtví jsou na čihadle
Čekají
Civí

Těžko je uspokojit
když jsou tak trpěliví

After Another Funeral

The crematory fire parted us
and the damp earth didn't help us reunite

He wasn't he was
She lived she died

The dead lurk around
Lie in wait
Glare

It's hard to appease them
since they've patience to spare

Milostná

Ležíš jako neživá
V té krajině za lží
Tvé vypouklé zrcátko
Mým dechem se zamží

Komentář určený méně zběhlým čtenářům poezie:

Básník se dívá na svou milou, která leží jako mrtvá,
skoro nedýchá. Není divu: prožila něco krásného a
silného—akt lásky, jenž napošpiní žádná lež. Básníka
upoutá milenčino bříško—potaženo lehounkou
lesklou blankou potu—připomíná mu vypouklé
zrcátko. Vzpomene si: kdesi četl, že pomocí kapesního
zrcátka lze zjistit přítomnost dechu u zdánlivě
mrtvého. Básník přikleká a v erotickém zmatku
silně dýchá na milenčino bříško. Teprve poté, co
se ubezpečil, že je nepochybně zamžené, bez obav
odchází do vedlejší místnosti napsat o zmíněné
události báseň. Přečtěte si ji nyní znovu!

Love Poem

In the land beyond lies
you lie as if lifeless
Your convex mirror
mists over with my breath

Commentary for readers less well-versed in poetry:

A poet gazes at his lover who lies there as if dead,
barely breathing. It's no wonder; she's experienced
something of great beauty and power—the act of love
that no lie can defile. He's captivated by the film of
glistening perspiration on his lover's belly. It reminds
him of a convex mirror. He recalls the time he once
read that with the help of a convex mirror you could
tell if an apparent corpse were still breathing. The
poet sinks to his knees and overcome by passion he
exhales deeply against his lover's belly. Once he's been
assured that there's no doubt that it's been covered
over in mist, he goes, without the slightest hesitation,
into the adjoining room to write about what inspired
the aforementioned poem. Now read it again!

Mlha je mlha je mlha

1.

Nebude ježíšek není kdy
Odložíme ho na nikdy
V krku se vzpříčila kůstka
Vypršela nám propustka
Nebude ježíšek fíky a slova
Všechno se skončí
A všechno začne znova
Mlha je mlha je mlha

2.

Zapálíme františka
Uděláme ježíška
Máme maso my se máme
Už si ladem uléháme
Do peří a do peřin
Město dáví slzný plyn
Mlha je mlha je mlha

Už tě svlékám jemně z kůže
Už už pukám jako bůžek
V dýmajících zrcadlech
Roste krápník tvůj můj dech
Už jsem na kost obnažený
Už jsem ženou obnožený
Už jsem jenom v pohybech

Fog Is Fog Is Fog

1.

We won't have another Christmas
We've put away our Baby Jesus
A fishbone's stuck in our throats
All our passports have been revoked
No more Christmas figs and grog
Everything has its terminus
To begin again anon
Fog Is Fog Is Fog

2.

We'll stoke the fire with another log
And do Christmas up whole hog
We have meat life's so sweet
Later on we'll all lie down
In our beds of eiderdown
The city belches tear gas now
Fog is fog is fog

Gently I have flayed your skin
I'm a laughing Buddha my sides split
From our breath stalagmites grow
In mirrors filled with smoke
I'm stripped naked and exposed
Wife-worn right down to the bone

Už se bude ryba kostit
Jenom nože budou hosty
Budou tišší málo ují
S lítostí mne rozporcují
A pak půjdou do peřin

3
Město dáví slzný plyn

The fish will then debone its flesh
Knives are our only dinner guests
They'll quietly eat a little bit
Dole me out and yet rue it
Then return to their eiderdowns

3
The city belches tear gas now

Sýčkování

Co když mám vážně seno v hlavě
Když pálím jednu za druhou
A k vínu přikusuju líh?
Co když jsem vážně chycený v té síti?

A seno v hlavě
V krvi líh
Zápalky v kapse
Jednoho dne se prostě samovznítí?!

Doom Foretold

What if there's really straw in my head
When I light up one cigarette after the next
And what if I sip my booze like wine
What if they've already set me up?
And straw in my head
Blood full of booze
Matches in my pocket
One day I'll simply self-combust!

Chvála čtyřtaktního těla

i like my body when it is with your
body. It is so quite new a thing.
—e.e. cummings

Mám rád své tělo
protože drží pohromadě
zatímco všechno okolo se rozpadá

Údy se vytrčují
zuby klapou
jazyk směs rozděluje
hrdlo nasává

A když se přes den obchodím
dohrkám domů na tři válce
usnu a tělo
už s ránem samo domluví
zda
a kde
dojde k nutné generálce

In Praise of the Four-Stroke
Internal Combustion Body

i like my body when it is with your
body. It is so quite new a thing.
—e.e. cummings

I like my body
because it holds together
while everything around me falls apart now

My limbs jut out
my teeth chatter
my tongue dishes up a mess
my throat sucks it down

And if all day I've been running around
I'll rattle home on three cylinders
I'll fall asleep and my body
by daybreak will announce
whether or not
and where
it will get the necessary repairs

Kámasútra

Dnes dám si nohu za ucho
poučen o rozkoši
a plynule a žádný chvat
vyměním svoji kůži hroší
za saténový duplikát

A pokazím
Kuřáckou záduchou
ten dlouhý strmý pád
do spánku
do terénu
který je bez okolí...

Dnes dám si nohu za ucho
a zapomenu
co kde
a proč
mne bolí

Kamasutra

Today I'll put my leg behind my head
Now I'm wise to passion
Without haste or hesitation
I'll trade my thick skin in
for a duplicate in satin

I'll do myself in
with my smoker's cough
The long sheer plunge
into dreams
into the region
that has no outskirts...

Today I'll put my leg behind my head
and forget
what where
and why
it hurts

O mladičké přadleně

(Janu Zábranovi)

Proměněná v loutku
najednou ožije...jen pro tu chvíli
než nitkou kouře v Rudém koutku
chytí pavoučka...než do střepu

zrcátka mrkne a honem zpátky poslepu
číst úvodník z osnovy tkalcovského stavu:
nemyslí na nic...myslí ať pukne
(mistr jenž v sále s temněrudým suknem

vyslídí u stropu viselce dýmu)
Neboť je léto v Rudém koutku
kam holka proměněná v loutku

chodí na tajnou cigaretu
aniž by tušila co vy čtenáři pohádek už víte:
že překročení zákazu smiřuje pošetilost s mýtem

About the Girl Mill Worker

*(For Jan Zábrana)**

Suddenly she springs to life
transformed into a puppet... only for the instant
when she traps a spider in the Red Party Shrine****
with a thread of smoke...before she eyes

her reflection a mirror shard and again blind
she reads the warp's editorial in the textile:
she thinks of nothing... until the foreman in the room
with crimson curtains blows his fuse

when he sees the smoke from her cigarette rise
For it's summer in the Red Party Shrine
where the girl-turned-puppet on the sly

slips out for a smoke and doesn't yet surmise
what you readers of fairytales already know so well:
folly reconciles with myth when you break the rules

---

* Jan Zábrana (1931–1984). Poet and distinguished translator of American and Russian poetry and prose, as well as an essayist.

** "...the Red Party Shrine". The red shrine (rudý koutek) refers to the place in a state-run building that was devoted to the glorification of the Communist Party.

Beerspective

(Janu Lopatkovi)

Koncem léta začátkem sedmdesátých
nebo osmdesátých let
vyšel jsem z Brčálky
což je hostinec ve čtvrti zvané Josefov
kde z mála slov vedl jsem
mnoho nejrůznějších řečí
zatímco opodál k zadnímu traktu
právnické fakulty
dorazil autobus s nimrody
po neposlední leči
a tak vešel jsem znovu do Brčálky
kde koncem léta
začátkem sedmdesátých
nebo osmdesátých let
obrácená sklenice je triedr
kterým lze blízké vidět zdálky

Beerspective

*(For Jan Lopatka)**

At summer's end at the beginning of the Seventies
  or Eighties
I left Brčalka a pub and eatery
in section of the city
called Josefov
using few words I carried on
discussions all and sundry
while nearby at law school of Charles University
a bus of hunters arrived at its rear wing
after their neither last nor final feast
and so once again I retreated
to Brčalka to drink and eat
where at summer's end
at the beginning of the Seventies
or Eighties
an overturned beer mug's the telescope
you use to view from afar what's near

---

* Jan Lopatka (1940–1993). Influential literary critic and editor. From 1969
  to 1989, Lopatka only published in samizdat and was an editor of samiz-
  dat books and magazines.

Laskavá normalizace

(Blance)

Je pozdní odpoledne laskavého léta a ty jdeš
navštívit přítelkyni Nad pískovištěm svítí
prach a dvě hočičky v bílých ponožkách visí
na kovové konstrukci hlavou dolů jako květiny
normalizace.

Je pozdní odpoledne laskavého léta a strážný
v kukani Československého rozhlasu hlavu
na prsou klímá jako sedlák po senoseči
normalizace.

Je pozdní odpoledne laskavého léta a tak
řekneš své přítelkyni hlavu vzhůru a vracíš
se zase parkem kde dvě holčičky visí hlavou
dolů jako květiny v bílých ponožkách
normalizace.

Sweet Normalization

*(For Blanka)**

It's a late afternoon in sweet summer and you're off
to see your girlfriend And the grit shines above the
    sandbox
while two little girls in white socks
hang upside down on the jungle gym's bars like
    blossoms
of normalization.

It's a late afternoon in sweet summer and the guard
at Radio Prague dozes head lolling to his chest
like a peasant after harvesting the crops
of normalization.

It's a late afternoon of this sweet summer and so
chin up you tell your friend and you go back again
through the park where two little girls hang upside
down like blossoms in the white socks
of normalization.

---

* **Blanka Stárková.** Fellow student of Šrut's at Charles University and
translator from Spanish. During normalization she worked for Spanish
section of Czech Radio. After 1989, she became Managing Editor for
Czech Radio's culture, classics and art station. She has translated García
Márquez, Borges, and other influential Spanish writers.

Acknowledgments

I AM DEEPLY INDEBTED TO THOSE PEOPLE AND ORGANIZA-tions that supported my efforts over several years to bring this collection to readers. This book would not have been possible without Michael Henry Heim and the PEN Translation Fund Grant he funded anonymously during his lifetime, the grant that, after his death, bears his name and speaks to his great contribution to literature and literature in translation. In memoriam to the person who did so much to break the glass ceiling of the three percent and bridge the divide among writers, translators. I am also most grateful for the generous support I received from The National Endowment for the Arts. Without the Translation Fellowship, I would never have been able to take the time I needed in Prague to complete the manuscript. I am also indebted to David Shook at Phoneme Media, who had the faith to put Pavel's vision into print, with the help of Phoneme's fiscal sponsor, PEN Center USA. To my dear friend, Ron Morosan, whose wonderful artwork graces this cover. It's been a joy to work together. To my wonderful friends—Vladimír Pech, Jiřina Kastlová and Galina Miklínová—whose love and support during the writing/translation process gave me the confidence to keep going when it didn't seem like the book would see the light of day. And, finally, to my husband, Bob, head cheerleader and keeper of the flame whenever mine was flagging. Much love, always.